To D.

frying as was said about someone — "Grace Under Pressure"

Best Wishes

Judy

THE WIND TURNING PAGES

Poems by

Judith Slater

OUTRIDERS POETRY PROJECT

Buffalo, NY 2011

Published by
Outriders Poetry Project
314 Highland Avenue
Buffalo, NY 14222

ISBN-13: 978-0-9841772-2-6
ISBN-10: 0-9841772-2-1

The following poems have previously appeared elsewhere as noted: "In the Black Rock Tavern," *Prairie Schooner* (Fall 2004), reprinted in *Readers' Digest* (March 2009); "The Deer," *AGNI Online* (December 2006); "Another hard frost," *Poet Lore* (Spring 2006); "Final Wishes," *The Chautauqua Literary Review* (2007); "The Great Round," *5AM poetry* (Spring 2007); "Jessie" and "As Autumn," *Prairie Schooner* (Spring 2008); "The Beauty," *Passager* (2008); "Adopted at Birth," *MARGIE* (2008); "Seduction," *The Minnesota Review* (2008); "Burial," *Sow's Ear* (Summer 2008); "Negro College Basketball Player Captured in Harlem," *MARGIE* (2009); "In the Northern Hemisphere," *Connecticut Review* (Fall 2009).

The assistance of Katka Hammond and Matt Schmidt in preparing this book for publication is gratefully acknowledged.

Front cover art: Catherine Parker, *September* (2007).
Courtesy of the artist, photo by Todd Treat.

Back cover photograph: Susan Haney

THE WIND TURNING PAGES

For Jerry, Susan and Dan

*

and for
Helen Conkling,
my comrade in poetry
for over thirty years

TABLE OF CONTENTS

I

ADOPTED AT BIRTH

Adopted at Birth

No, I was not, as I was told,
born in a rooming house, red
and scabby, held under a faucet
and slathered with olive oil
before being handed over.

No, I was born in a trampled bed
of ferns and shot into the world
glistening. A tongue cleaned me.
A moist nose nudged me upright.
That night, I watched lights
blinking around us and thought
I will like this place.

Believe me when I tell you
I ran before I learned to walk
properly, took the stairs at a bound,
my new parents behind me,
cautious, "One at a time, Miss."

In neighborhood games,
my legs tangled hopelessly,
but, alone in woods, I leapt ravines,
rooted and rolled freely.

When I came upon a doe and fawns,
we exchanged long looks. Once,
against the fiery screen of sunset,
a massive stag blocked my path.

The House on Lake Erie

I grew in the shadow of crosses carved over doors
to ward off witches, slept in a canopied bed
with a cradle beneath. Outside my window
in the garden was the grave of a servant's child.

I held my breath passing the cellar door,
although once, pressed behind my brother,
I descended to find the tunnel
where runaway slaves had been hidden.

I loved the chambered attic with its trunks
of christening clothes and beaded gowns,
mahogany bureaus stuffed with hand-stitched linens,
astonishing wreaths of women's hair.

Sickly, sleeping in the south wing
its air thought to be healthier, was I,
as they claimed, born skittish? or was I
shaped by nights marooned in a high bed,

fingers of evergreens stroking the windows,
murmurs snaking through floor boards,
and between me and the other sleepers,
corridors with inky stairwells?

Seduction

Seven and in love for life with my uncle
at the wheel of a Ford convertible—
sun glasses, slicked-back hair, movie star profile.

We've dropped off my aunt to shop
and are traveling at a speed that would horrify
my parents. He's teasing, bets me 50 cents

he knows the color of my underpants.
"They're shocking pink," he shouts into the wind.

I raise my riffling skirt. "They're white," I yell.

"I lose," he grins. "I'll buy the ice cream."
At a picnic table beside Chautauqua Lake,
I make up stories to hold his attention,

but his veiled eyes look across the lake to the casino
where every weekend he and my aunt
drink and dance and celebrate the end of war.

"They'll ruin themselves," my mother says.
And they do.

First Death

In the hushed room with velvet drapes,
organ music, disturbing perfumes,
I grip my father's hand.
We walk up to the gleaming box,
the satin-chambered profile.
He drops my hand and strokes
his mother's forehead. "Like sleep,"
he says and lifts me up to touch.
A stone. No, colder. I scream
and go on screaming.
In the car, tucked in a lap robe,
snow thickly falling, the radio playing,
I catch his smoke rings on my fingers.
Like sleep. Like smoke. Like snow.

A crimson berry

> on the bush beside my coffee cup flares
in morning sunlight, and I'm transported
to a farm that's disappeared, an aunt

on the kitchen porch, an uncle in shadows
in the barn door. In country voices,
they call my name, tell me to find my cousins.

One's pitching hay to black and white cows
and holds a halter so I can lay my cheek against
the bony flank, feed grass to bristly soft lips.

Her name is Daisy.

Soon a day comes when I follow him
into the concrete building behind the barn,
past shackled cows to where blood, the odor

of iron, swirls into drains, and headless bodies
hang from hooks. When I slump, a man
in a black rubber apron says, "Jesus!"

But today, memory is under the sway of sunlight,
and my cousin in the tranquil pasture
hoists me on his shoulders. We jog off to find his sister.

Country Girls

School over, we burst into summer,
careening down hills on bicycles, no brakes.
And we go nearly naked in halters,
shorts, no underwear. Skin blistered,
then browned, feet sticky black with tar,
we're dog-spider-wasp-and-snake-bitten,
horse-thrown, skunk-sprayed, Bee Bee-stung,
Indian-burned. Daring each other, we leap off
shed roofs and cliffs, swim out deep,
until one summer—who can remember which?
we begin to dab tropical colors on lips and nails,
smudge our lids with purple eye shadow.

Jessie

Touch the electric fence, she commands. *Swallow frog spit.*
Crawl under the bull's belly. Round up the captives.

I collect them—Dottie, Chuck, Pauline, my brother—
and lead them blindfolded through our woods
to the abandoned shed, where I push them
up rotting stairs to the airless attic littered
with mildewed magazines, loud with bees.

She teeters on a stack of crates, torso stained
with iodine, buzzard feathers in a bandanna
around her head. The captives kneel.
I pass around a cup of purplish liquid.
Lion's blood for courage, she thunders, tossing me
a wink. Eyes of fallen sky, warrior cheekbones.
Never again a glance compelling as hers.

The last day, we swam the reservoir, sprawled
on the bank, packing mud on mosquito bites.
Suddenly she grabbed a forked stick
and thrust it at me, jeering:
this is what men look like down there
poking it sharply between thumb and forefinger
 this is what they do to you.
                    "You're lying!" I cried.
You just wait!

The next day, she didn't come out, but I found her
curled on her bed, legs bloodied by a thrashing.
Then she disappeared and it was rumored
she'd run off with a farm worker. Heartbroken,
I seemed to see her everywhere, disappearing
down a school corridor, running in the far pasture,
looking over her shoulder for me.

That morning

                 when we were fifteen, I started out to meet you,
cardinals whistling up their mates, ditches
gleaming with the gelatin of frogs' eggs,
and everywhere in the day's noisy industry,
like mushrooms after rain, boys—

lugging milk cans, pitching hay, driving
cows, forklifts, tractors, roaring past
in pickup trucks. And the one who,
brakes screeching, gears grinding,
shot back in reverse and patted

the cracked leather seat beside him.
A boy with a buzz cut, a fullback's
broken nose, who knew the tractor trails
and swerved off-road, grinning
as the truck lunged like a rodeo bull,

handing me the wheel just as he
jammed down on the accelerator
and, you'll understand, there was no help for it
but to steer toward the willow grove,
breathing in hay and sweat and cigarette smoke.

"Loose Women"

I pictured them lounging on stoops
with cigarettes and pop cans.
I knew that once you loosened your legs,
you had to give up hope of a white wedding gown.
It was surprising, then, to find myself
falling back on a leather jacket,
the night sky crowning a dark head,
and wanting what I'd been warned against—
whatever it took to be loosened.

July, Long Light

At five years, I had to come in at night
before the others who went on playing
Capture the Flag as I hung out the window
pretending the elm's shadow was a ladder.
When I was fifteen, James Dean loitered
in light rays as I drifted through summer dusks.
Then came nights when I melted into shadows
with this one or that one. Later, children,
who were put to bed so I could slip out,
knowing the ladder depended on an angle of sun
and on there being only a sliver of time.

Amazing

—for Susan

The summer we strolled beside Loch Lomond,
then crossed to Norway, saw the Viking boats,
you, a continent away, rocked in secret waters.
In Sweden, we admired the beauty of children
with no knowledge of your face, which by then
had its distinctive curve of cheek, almond eyes.

We were back in England at Oxford
when the one who bore you felt labor pangs.
Were you moving down your birth canal
the day we boated on the Thames?
And when you took your first breath
was I looking down at the Colleges

thinking only of what lay below me?
Ignorant of a moment that awaited when,
arriving home, we'd receive a call
and follow down a corridor to a room,
a crib, and you, six weeks old,
smiling up as though you knew us.

Risk

—for Dan

The crow looks like it's having fun
taking short quick steps on the frozen creek
and sliding, step, step, slide.
It doesn't seem desperate, but pecks at the ice
as if seeing grains under the transparency.
Then it's joined by another and another
until there are dozens skating among the trees.
The sky darkens and they fly into it—
all but one who continues skating
even as a curtain of sleet billows over the ice.
I think, son, of you who relishes storms.

Family Vacation

Four weeks in, quarreling and far
from home, we came to the loneliest place.
A western railroad town. Remember?
I left you at the campsite with greasy pans
and told our children not to follow me.
The dying light had made me desperate.
I broke into a hobbled run, across tracks,
past warehouses with sun-blanked windows
to where a playground shone in a wooded clearing.
Then I was swinging, out over treetops.
I saw myself never going back, yet
whatever breathed in the mute woods
was not another life. The sun sank.
I let the swing die, my toes scuffed earth,
and I was rocked into remembrance
of the girl who had dreamed the life I had.
Through night, dark at the root, I returned to it.

When the children were young,

        I admit, there were times I wished they were older.
Now I'm alone in a room with clean windows,
cardinals feeding on hawthorn berries,
sparrows hobnobbing in the bushes.
I find myself pacing, tugging at my hair,
considering-without-seeing my image
in the mirror. Then I let the dog out,
run a bare foot over the cat on the rug,
shake yellow leaves off the fig plant.
Another cup of tea. *Sit still*, I tell myself
in a tone I used with the children
which prompts me to call one of them,
wistful for their interruptions, the way
imagination wove around them.

Summer Night

Cigarette smoke from a porch
where a young neighbor plays
Madonna on her boom box

and lazily calls her children.
Ain't no big deal...
Tonight no one will hurry in.

Smoke from a bonfire where men,
beer cans aloft, raise raspy voices:
Feelin' good was easy, Lord...

I call up the stairs and you promise "soon,"
but not wanting to miss anything,
I walk out alone, past lighted porches

with couples playing cards, girls
clustered on steps, children
darting in and out of shadows.

An old man, bare chest, loose white hair,
holds a hose over his tomato vines.
"Good Evening, Miss," he calls.

Miss! I smile and wave, glad
to be walking on two good legs,
to be a part of it, to hear you behind me.

Ordinary Transformations

Love wakes me with its sweet dishevelment
and I embrace its pleasure, then rise
to a quiet house. Where once was hubbub—
children, pets, both of us off to work—
now is time, transparency.

I watch an old woodchuck in the lettuces
who turns a conspirator's eye: *we both know
how delicious these taste*—and I do know.
I think if I hurry to the creek, a heron
may lift from the shallows and I'll finish a poem,

but I chat with a neighbor, come home
to messages; then it's time to peel, chop, bread, sauté,
to place a dish before the man who for nearly 50 years
has mostly relished what I've given him.
We share the day's events, the world's.

Maybe a movie, an hour of *Grand Illusion*, say,
before we both drift off, and when, on the rim
of sleep, the night wind ruffles my hair,
I yield to its embrace, to the solitary journey.

II

ELEGY

Bride Descending a Staircase, 1925

The Rogerson residence transforms
into an autumn bower: great baskets
of gladioli, delphinium, asters, liatris,
wild clematis wound around balustrades.
The bride descends in her gown of ivory crepe,
veil of princess lace, her slippers white satin
with tiny sprigs of orange blossoms.
She wears a bracelet set with diamonds
and emeralds, a gift from her father.

The Hands They Pledge

She brings the graces of her finishing school,
the dark genes of her Scottish father, a body
she struggles with, a gift for devotion.

He, a butcher's son with many brothers,
brings pranks and jollity, a taste for fashion,
surprisingly soft hands.

Snapshot, 1926

She stands a step behind him,
holding his arm, her body concealed
under a Chinese shawl. He engages
the camera with a smile—straw hat,
white knickers, legs akimbo.
He likes plump women, thin ones too.

Adores them all. But she is not at ease
at dances and afternoon teas in gauzy gowns,
Sundays in the First Presbyterian family pew.
Except for sighs, she keeps her feelings close.
We watch her shoulders quiver over the sink
and fail to understand what troubles her,

while he for whom life is a snap
of the fingers, a jingle of coins
in his pocket, whistles through his days
and nights. Summer evenings, she slips
away from us to tend her gardens.
His laughter blows in from adjacent lawns.

After Her Nap

4:30 p.m. The Baby Ben clamors.
She rises in a series of hesitations,
body unwilling as water,
sprinkles talc on her girdle,
inches it up, sighs,
and falls back on the bed.
Gathers a nylon stocking
over a calloused foot,
rolling it up, snapping it,
front, side, and back.
Ducks her head into a dress
that falls in whispers
over a taffeta slip, and pins
her hair in a French roll.
Steps into heels, rouges
cheeks and lips, sprays
Emeraude, clips on
a necklace, matching earrings.
5:30. She descends to the kitchen
where she's left vegetables peeled,
meat seasoned, cake frosted,
table set. She ties on an apron,
ready for him to come home.

Zippo

I didn't think *handsome* then, I thought
my father the way he saunters down Main Street,
housewives, shopkeepers, mechanics calling out,
children running up to get Lifesavers. The way
he pauses to chat, flipping his lighter open,
tamping the Lucky Strike on his thumbnail.

I sneak into his den when he's out, tuck
into the kneehole of his desk and sniff
his Zippo until dizzy, emboldened;
then play little tricks, mixing red and black
inks in his fountain pen, twisting together
paperclips. If I lift the telephone receiver

quietly, I can listen in on our party line.
That's how I hear two women
talking about him. That's why my mother
finds me that night sleepwalking, sobbing.
"It's all right," she tells me,
"you had a nightmare, come to bed."

Her sighs

are stings that wake us
when the garden
groans to be picked.
They curdle the cream
on berries set out
for the last one up,
locate a child
behind a door
draped around a book,
and track our father
on his errands,
seeding the clouds
where he turns in
at the Legion.
Her sighs make bread
rise, pickle cucumbers.
They lard her laughter
when we've teased her
into playfulness.
Evenings, she sits mending
and they ascend
with gentle regularity
into the circle of lamplight.

Afterglow

Buttery, whispery, impossibly
high tenor voices, tobacco-y, overripe,
snake into our living room—the Platters,
Four Freshmen, cryin' Johnny Ray.
My father feigns convulsions.
He likes the old smoothies—Bing, Perry

and teases when I have friends over,
replacing my record with Guy Lombardo.
Then he grabs my reluctant mother
and springs from the kitchen in a foxtrot
while I burn with shame. At the way
he twitches his hips, at my friends' silence.

Toward the end of his life, visiting him
in the Manor, I attend dances, seated
behind the wheelchairs, my eyes welling,
as he dances with the exercise teacher
and all the residents who can stand,
his bad leg dragging, but his hips

keeping the rhythm. Aides wink at him.
Two times around on *Peg O' My Heart*
and I'm persuaded to join. He leads me
in a foxtrot, a waltz, a bunny hop.
We make chicken noises in a circle.
It's heady. We dance so freely.

Soon

        the stories you and I preserve, brother,
will be dust on the antique table, on the photograph
of the young man with a mustache, the demure bride.
The mother I remember sits alone,
red-hot tip of a cigarette inscribing the darkness.

Yours tells you secrets, ruffles your hair.
When you die, the bridegroom with a too-ready
smile, the girl dewy with future tears, will vanish.
When I die, so will the charming man, the weary woman,
the guise of a *long happy marriage*. Only their solitary dusts....

Grace Rogerson, 1905-1969

Not as on that day of surgeons and the body's betrayal.
I would have you be a flower in the subtle fields
of fall when pods are opening in a final beauty—
sleepy catchfly, shepherd's purse, sweet cicely,
the pearly everlasting, blue heal-all.

Reynold (Bud) Fairbank, 1906-1986

The day after, driving to the hospital
for your Bulova watch and cameo ring,
I saw you—swinging in a doughnut-shaped cloud.
Outside the bedroom window at dusk, a bird
chipped like your old Zippo with the worn flint
and I leaned out to search the garden for the flare
of a cigarette. I set the gold watch on the bed stand
and thought of the years it had measured out
your vigorous days. Then I went soundly to sleep.

Birth Mother

The wind is harsh in this cemetery.
Only a small group has gathered
for the burial of her ashes.

Sixty years ago, she handed me over
without remembering my sex
or the color of my hair.
A red-haired boy, she told the man she wed.

But I looked and found her in later years
and was pleased to notice
her nose and brow were like mine,
as was her quickness to cry.

When she lay in a nursing home, her brain
unraveling, I'm told that she grasped the arm
of a stranger and pulled him to her, whispering,
"I've been a good girl."

I think of an April day when she, nineteen,
alone in a boarding house,
knew it was time and walked to a hospital.

Each of us places a rose on the grave.
Now when it's too late, I long to offer her
a child's fistful of dandelions,
sleep in the curve of her body.

III

THE GREAT ROUND

Prologue

—after Primo Levi's *Periodic Table*

These blazing leaves
driven to earth by rain
are on their way
underground
where carbon in an orange leaf
lights up the intestines
of an earthworm,
dissolves and makes its way
through to the ocean
to be trapped for centuries
in a coral reef
or fly for years
with the wind
before rapping on the door
of a ginkgo tree.
Even the atoms of a kiss
may penetrate the heart.

April

A shake of the drake's tail
as he mounts his mate says it.
So does the squirrel swinging
in the tree's high hammock,
the groundhog sitting erect
with crossed paws—
here is green breeze
no heart will hide from.
And you, cave dweller,
perpetually pulsing,
you, too, syncopate your beat.

A May Walk with the Ornithological Society

They'd risen before daybreak, camouflaged
themselves in black and olive green
and, silent, flocked behind their leader.
The least birder among them knew

this was the week for the five-inch penny-weight
transients—the Blue-winged, Bay-breasted,
the Chestnut-sided, Yellow-rumped,
Cape May, Magnolia, Cerulean.

A man who lagged behind called to them,
teakettle teakettle and *weeta weeta weeteo*
along with *chek chek chek,* and birds
seemed to pause to give him back his song.

"Doesn't he know," a woman said,
"they have no time to spare?"
Two months traveling, bodies spent,
and with a Great Lake yet to cross.

She'd stood on the far shore
with tourists from around the world
to watch the birds alight, a golden cloud.
Some dropped in the lake and drowned.

Woodchuck

Ten years
in your burrow under my deck
you've lived alone.

Through winter,
I think of you under the floorboards,
under the thrum

of the furnace,
under frozen earth,
resting upright in a ball,

knowing that come March
you'll again climb the deck
and hold my gaze until I turn away.

This spring, you have a mate.
I fear expansion of your tunnels,
mean to call the "Trapper with a Heart,"

but reminisce about our long relationship,
the way our clocks are synchronized,
the nightly ritual of your solemn gaze.

Enduring Sir,
let us consider compromise.
Send off your family. Fill in tunnels.

Two ought to do for a bachelor.
For my part, I'll agree to the slight sinking
that takes me deeper into earth.

Bee Sting

The time I wandered through a field
gold and humming to its far horizon
trailed by a baby who pulled off flower heads
to offer me, I dreaming along, not listening
to her babble, the little screeches, until
a tiny hand on my leg alerted me
to a fiery swollen face, a wheezing chest.
I carry still the weight of her as of one
vanished beyond calling whose return
depended on my pounding feet and breath.

Lake Vacation

Into our campfire last night, into our circle
where we were riddling riddles, leapt the cat,
yowling, springing into laps, frantically

rubbing its cheeks against each of us.
We petted it in turn as the nearly full moon
pooled in the lake and the youngest fell asleep.

All night, stalking the windows, the cat cried.
Each time I woke, I hoped not to hear it.
In her bedroom, my daughter tossed,

her daughter came in from the tent, weeping:
"The cat...I can't sleep."
This morning I'll go to houses but I won't

find its owner. My last cat claimed me in a cemetery,
a mere mite mewling like a jaybird. *No more pets,*
I said when it died. Today we depart.

With charred sticks, the children write their names
on the dock. I find a box for the inconvenient cat.
What we will we see each other through!

After Frost

On a radiant afternoon, a yellow leaf
detaches and descends,

crosses the ascending arc of a goldfinch
and rests near a Black-eyed Susan

where a swallowtail pulses its ragged
tiger-striped wings and a diaphanous

orange and yellow leaf-hopper chews.
Leaf, petal, wing: the moment's genius.

In the Northern Hemisphere

A matter of hours and the white moth
flitting around my flowered blouse
will curl on the ground.
So will the red leaf twirling on its stem.

A Magnolia Warbler pauses to feed.
Soon it will join others in the night sky—
black shadow
sweeping the moon's face.

A doe has lain down with her babies,
as I used to. Their jaws slide slowly
side to side. A few months
and they will be ripping at bark.

As Autumn

                approaches with its subtle alloy
of burnish and tarnish,

we watch the crows at light-fall,
hundreds, maybe thousands

flocking to a roost,
the air full of brazen alarms, near-

collisions, noisy settlings
and re-settlings.

Tree limbs shake and tremble.
This could be an army in tight

formation or a massing of refugees,
abundance or the hard edge of famine.

On every branch of every tree,
darkness, and silence.

Another hard frost

                and the garter snake soaking in weak sun
will slide underground to wind in a knot with others.
We'll pull out flannel sheets and, mornings,
turn up the heat to dress—
with little memory of the night's descent,
the press of limbs that guides us back.

November and a light snow falling

"Hunters' snow," you say, remembering
when you woke before dawn
to meet your deer-hunting friends

and Betty at the diner served up eggs
and sausage, home fries, and biscuits.
Filled your thermoses with free coffee.

I help you name them: Shorty, Ed, Cliff,
Meryl, and one you can't remember,
although he never missed a season.

You were tall those years, coming
up the driveway at dusk,
and we ran to unlace your boots.

Small now, lopsided in a wheelchair,
you raise your watch ceremoniously
to blind eyes.

I was a lover of nursery tales
when I first thrust my hands
into your game pocket,

felt cold fur, a stiff body.
You laid the rabbit out
on the butcher block.

I stood as close as I dared
while you stripped off the skin
as one would remove gently

a baby's snowsuit, peeling it
down the legs, pulling it
inside out over the tiny feet.

Your feet are swollen
and purple. I look away
when nurses change the dressings.

Northern Thanksgiving

A day of scant light. Men hunt, toss footballs;
children, free until dinner, scatter.
A day to polish silver, wipe off the good china.
Lonely, if you're without the company
of women who taught you the way of it.

One will phone when her bird's in the oven.
You'll remember other Thanksgivings, like
the one when Grandmother bolted from the table
into a snowstorm. She enjoyed upstaging
her daughters, but that time, wasn't she

expressing what they too felt—the thanklessness
of preparing a feast consumed in an hour?
Granted, amidst the rivalries, drinking,
and overeating, there were moments—
when you held hands and a child said grace.

Or, after dinner when you gathered in the kitchen
to pick at the carcass and tell stories, the favorite
being the chase after Grandmother, with children
and dogs tumbling, you yourselves like children
running coatless, wild, into the season's first snow.

Christmas Afternoon

—for Jerry

The same time as always,
we walk out with the black dog.
She's all that is visible in the storm.
Caps pulled down to eyeglasses,
we trudge as she leaps and leaps,
blooms of snow riding her sleek back.

We talk of other years,
of the red dog and the yellow dog,
of our children in fluorescent snowsuits,
the mothers who muffled us in scarves.
Crows are screaming. We can just
make them out, wheeling over evergreens.

We are arctic, strange
shapes in a dissolving landscape.
I shiver and lean into you, feel
your arm tighten around me. The crows
settle. The young dog bounds forward.

Smokers in Winter

They nod, standing outside my office,
men stamping feet, women clutching
cardigans across their chest, shifting
from one high heel to the other.
Some mornings, their faces blush
with faint sun; on others, wind
drives them into a huddle.
A man steps out to hold the door
as I juggle lunch bag and briefcase.
I envy their intimacy with the day's
fugitive light, and, though I'd like to,
I can't buy a pack of my old Marlboros,
put on a short skirt and join them.
After dark, though, when I walk out
into the empty parking lot, I'll pause
where they stood to enjoy snow whirling
like smoke in the halo of the streetlamp.

The Dreamer

Long leafless winter nights I lie down early,
release my mind and let the dreamer paint
her nightly scene. It may be waves will carry me,
as once they did, into a sparkling cove
where young John Keats poured out his song
that faded as the first light broke. I heard
myself speak words aloud: *Adieu. The fancy*
cannot cheat so well as she is famed
 to do and all that day I felt a hand
in mine and brimmed with leafy words.

The Deer

They bolt from their cover
in patchy trees, lots staked for development,
to shelter beside my leafless hedge—

five bony refugees of our suburb,
fleeing the woods where grain is bait
and official sharpshooters lurk.

Their ears twitch in my direction
but I must not feed them. More and more
would come, a preserve in my backyard.

Nights, I see them passing, wraithlike,
ripping at bark, balancing on hind legs
to nibble from the bird feeders,

pausing, first one, then the others,
to look toward the house
where I watch from behind the curtain.

One morning soon,

                            there'll be roistering cries
of geese flying north from the Chesapeake,
steered by memory of spring grasses.
They'll land to feed in our flooded backyard.
I'll pull on black stockings and boots to join them
in the transitory lake. Don't be surprised
if I come back with marsh weeds in my hair.

IV

STAR NURSERY

"Negro College Basketball Player Captured in Harlem"

—*NY Post*, 1958

Black as a tar pit, some said, black as Satan.
No, satin, I thought, when, in the cafeteria.
I couldn't take my eyes off his hands
engulfing the coffee cup or fingering scars on the table.
We cheered when he floated down the court,
swiveled past the defense, and dunked the ball.
Afterward, to tunes on the jukebox,
he wheeled girls out and sent them airborne.
We cheered some more.

He wanted to date us; we wanted to be friends.
So we were pleased when he
and the high-school daughter of a dean
fell in love and for a few weeks walked
arm in arm on campus before disappearing.
We woke to phone calls—magazines vying
for first-hand accounts, photographs.
He'd shot us into the national spotlight,
he was ours, and we rooted for them.

When his picture appeared in The Post
over the caption MANHUNT, we believed
they'd escape, right up to the AP photo
outside a theater where, eyes dazed,
he is shielding her from police. We wondered
if he'd gone to prison, if she'd waited for him.
We asked about him at reunions.
Years later someone reported meeting him.
He had a degree in engineering, worked for DuPont.

Sunday Fishermen, Lake Erie

They could be in church at prayer
for all they move or speak,

lined up along the railing
in old workpants and flannels,

hunched over their poles.
From time to time, they probe

their bait pails, light
a cigarette, lift a thermos.

Tomorrow, outfitted in hard hats
and safety glasses, they may be

running drill presses, driving
bulldozers, swinging wrecking balls,

may be working double shifts
on road crews, holding up signs: Stop, Go.

Someone turns to rest his back
against the railing, staring

into a distance, past
the jostle of the bike path.

In the Black Rock Tavern

The large man in the Budweiser tee
with serpents twining on his arms
has leukemia. They've told him
he won't die for years
if he sticks with the treatment.

He's talking about his days in the foundry
running a crane on an overhead track.
Ten hours a shift moving ingots into rollers.
Sometimes without taking a break
because of the bother of getting down.
Never had an accident.
He had that much control.

His problem was electricity
arcing through his body and accumulating.
When he got down at the end of a shift
he could squeeze a twenty-watt light bulb
between thumb and finger and make it flare.
He was famous for that.

Edward Hopper

He knew how to tint light
and brush it over a house, a landscape
so that we never forget:

"Hopper," we say, walking at dusk
past brick-red storefronts, windows
glazed by dying sun.

His humans seem to know they will never
be graced by love or good news —
like the ill-matched couple

in "Cape Cod Evening," their feet
sunk in glowing grasses,
she standing apart, eyes downcast,

he on the stoop, stretching an arm
toward a collie that looks away.
Dark pinewoods advance, one bough

stroking a shaded window, while light
without promise or soul dazzles the landscape
as it slides imperceptibly westward.

The Man in a Red Cap

All afternoon at the Whitney under Hopper's spell—
his vision of life without volition, I step out now
into the buzz of Madison Avenue. Across from me
in a blank brick façade, a window opens
and a man in a red cap looks out at the street
where taxis and cyclists dart, a bus lurches,
and dogs harnessed together propel their attendant
at a clip. The stream of walkers divides and flows
around nannies pushing strollers two abreast
who pause as a peddler unfurls yellow and blue
silk scarves. A doorman leaning on a taxi fender
cups his hands and shouts up. The man in the red cap
signals, and reappears in the street.

The Reed Cutter

—Iraq, 2004, *New York Times* photo feature

Here, poling his wooden skiff through rushes
of the Kirmashiya Marsh, is Mr. Abdullah
whose distant ancestors were Sumerians.

The clouded waters beneath his boat
rest between arms of the legendary
Tigris and Euphrates.

Mr. Abdullah holds up his hand,
maimed in a prison, declaring
it is doing again what it was meant to—

casting fishnets and cutting reeds for market.
He has come home with the help of a global
corps of engineers. Dams, built to expel

a dictator's enemies, are being torn down;
what was desert is again wide waters,
alive with reeds and cattails, fish and frogs.

For Mr. Abdullah, it is simple—
with more water, reeds will be thicker,
small silver fish and buffalo milk plentiful.

And although his family cannot yet drink the water,
although what lies ahead is unknown,
"This is what we call rebirth," he says.

"Have a Good Day"

(Iraq)

You are not the man
in the news clip
you saw this morning,

the one pacing
beside a row of sheeted forms
outside a marketplace:

That's my daughter,
number nine. Number seven
is my wife. May they
be fortunate.

Salam 'alaykom he may have said
to the shopkeeper upon leaving
to join his family in the bazaar.

You are not walking out
into the newsreel
you saw this morning.

Souvenir

—for EBF, teacher and friend

Spruce trees on the disappearing path
brush me closely when, late in your life,
I visit your house in the woods.
You move as if air itself were an obstacle,
but greet me with a young man's shyness
and with flowers and platters of food.

Wanting me to hear a new recording,
you place the needle with a trembling hand.
Cats lie on the carpet between us,
paws tucked, eyes narrowing in sleep.
In the half-light of the declining sun
your eyes shine like tapers.
Then the room is seized with music.
I raise a hand to your shoulder and we dance.

The Beauty

At sixteen, she married well—eighth child
of Swedish immigrants—had a cook and driver,
a governess for her children.

Grandmother of wardrobes and spicy tempers,
she kicked her leg over her head dancehall style
and perked up gatherings with fits and faintings.

Into her nineties, plump as a melon, she tended
her garden, an ornamental jumble where tomatoes
shone among rioting cosmos, and tethered

runner beans grew side by side with trellised roses.
No one could compete with the profusion of her hybrid teas
or the drenched blue of her delphinium.

At one hundred, she'd buried husband and children
without observable grief and lived imperiously
in a nursing home, each morning choosing an aide

to corset her, help her select jewelry. When the power
went out, she phoned the electric company to say
Mrs. Victor Campbell Rogerson wanted the lights on!

One hundred and two. Weary of clothes, she pulled them off
as soon as she was dressed, and, nearly naked
in a high-backed chair, conversed with the Queen of Sweden.

Once, when I took her hand, she yanked my fingers apart,
growling, "Because I've been hurt so much."
And her sunken blue eyes blazed.

Dead Sea Spa

Because I saw them from the bus
black-daubed figures
cavorting on the sands
bobbing in the salt-dense sea

and because I saw myself
transformed by mud
fabled restorative of
Cleopatra's silken skin—

that's how I came to be
naked on a gurney
in a tiled room,
flipped like a chicken

by a grim-faced attendant
who slathered me front
and back, wrapped me
mummy-tight in a plastic sheet,

and left without a word
of encouragement.
Long after I'd hardened
into a slab with darting eyes

she came to hose me down,
collect her fee.
How grateful I was to return
to my unperfected self.

As It Was in the Beginning

Eve: What a drag. You're beautiful, but tame
as the lions and all this lying down together
not to mention your lording it over me, well…
You think you're God's gift?
You're nothing but a glorified rib donor!

[*aside*] I can still feel the Other's powerful arms
when he lifted me out. Can't *wait* to see Him!
The Scaly One knows something.

*

Adam: So giddy, so full of yourself—
why can't you ever stay at home?
If you want variety, I'll rub you with fragrant oils.
Or, dress you up in vines
and then undress you.
But, no, you want the world.

*

God: I see it unfolding, eons of entertainment:
she will give birth to daughters who will give birth to
Helens and Cleopatras and violet-eyed Elizabeths.
The sons of her sons will pursue them,
pausing only to wage wars.
World without end? Don't ask *Me*!

Star Nursery

—for a grandchild

Somewhere in a galaxy
brilliant newborns nestle in whirling gases,
sparks whose light will arrive at our planet
tens of thousands of years from now.

Of all the small, already dying sparks
falling through the smoky golden swirl
we call the universe, I picture you—
drifting down through spacelessness

to settle briefly, curled and cradled
in salt waters, sailing through pre-history,
losing gills and tail, mitten hands meeting,
head nodding like a ghostly flower,

until, guided by the signal of your mother's
heartbeat, you approach our harbor,
arriving with your own question,
here, at our particular address.

The Worriers

You don't see this much anymore
except in certain neighborhoods.
Two women with silver-threaded hair in nets
face each other closely on the sidewalk,
plump arms hanging from sleeveless smocks,
bare legs in house slippers— the speaker
gesticulating, the listener, propping an elbow
in one hand, chin in the other. From time
to time they pause to clutch at each other
as if some morsel of news was painful to swallow.
It's about the children and grandchildren.
They stand in the summer heat and suffer.

Grandmothers on the Playground

See how they struggle after their charges
who tuck into cubbyholes. How, cheerfully,
they climb ladders to grab an overall strap,
bend their reluctant hinges and travel down a chute—
in pursuit. Even when they wallop their heads
or become wedged, they laugh like children.
Afterward, sitting on a bench, they call out:
Wait your turn! Take that out of your mouth!
Come over here and rest.

Painted Toenails

Glazed fire-engine red by my granddaughter,
their bravado led me all summer.
Time to wind up the charade,
strip them down to their pale originals
with lines like tree rings.

Ode to My Knees

Yesterday you carried me
up a small mountain.
Yet we were not together
and fell twice
even with the help
of two sticks.

Not long ago,
we were fleet,
first down hills
leaping
goat-footed,
Now you are bone
grating on bone.

Tomorrow, we'll wander
the streets of Manhattan,
hustled along
by the rush and press
of the Great Body,
resting with others
on benches in Central Park
and Washington Square.

If you should buckle
hurrying down steps
toward an arriving train,
strangers will catch us.
In the subway car
tough young men
will give up their seats.
In their eyes, we come from
the distant country of the frail.
Only you and I know the fervor
with which we go forth.

Wishes

I want to wake to a northern meadow
with pools of glittering snowmelt
and willows budding yellow beside
a stream's bright cresses.

Let all the greens be youthful,
suffused with sun and touched
with black in the trampled spaces
where deer lie down.

Let there be crows, and shadows
of crows, mushrooms and wild leeks
to gather, soup in an earthenware bowl—
two spoons.

Home with a Cold, Reading

Set me this day on a privileged path,
a wicker tray with toast and marzipans
and sugared tea in blue rose china cups.

Grant me long gazing out at flights of birds
and planes with purposeful trajectories
while the world goes on without me.

Let *Life stand still* as Mrs. Ramsey wraps
her shawl around Death's head. Draw down
the window shades with crocheted pulls

and bring me dreams of summer seas.
And treetops, let me fly.
Grant me slow waking to my place again.

EPILOGUE

The Wind Turning Pages

Wind rounds the corner of the sleeping house, swirls
down the chimney, through the rooms,
stirs the dreamer…

*

In a summer garden
under an elm tree,
the infant sleeps
in a wicker basket.
Cool breezes.

*

The birds discover her:
the house wren
drops to a low branch,
the cardinal whistles.

71

Sunday Drive

Father, in a fedora, whistles,
one hand on the wheel. The other

squeezes the hand of Mother
to keep her from slipping

away from us.
My brother, beside me

in the back, kicks at the seat.
I tie and retie a scarf to protect

my hairdo, inspect my image
in the rearview mirror.

Don't stick
Your elbow
Out so far
It might go home
In another car

"BURMA SHAVE!" we shout.
Even Mother.

Farm Boys

There I am on the cracked
leather seat of a pick-up
beside a straw-haired boy
who knows the tractor trails
and wheels off-road.
The truck pitches and rolls
like a rodeo bull
across the field
to a screen of willows.

First Love

(after Basho)

Even holding hands—
seeing you look away—
I long for you

Reprise: When the children were young,

I admit, there were times I wished they were older.
Now I'm alone in a room with clean windows.
Sit still, I tell myself in a tone I used then,
which prompts me to call one of them,
wistful for their interruptions, the way
imagination wove around them.

Putting up the hammock,

I remember the girl who dreamed a life
which is less than and more than
and exactly what she dreamed.

Reprise: Christmas Afternoon

We walk out into the heavy snowstorm.
The crows are screaming. I can just
make them out, wheeling over evergreens.
We are arctic, strange shapes in a dissolving
landscape. I shiver and lean into you.
The crows settle. The young dog bounds forward.

After Nearly 50 Years

He: You don't listen.
You repeat a phrase
and seconds later say *uh huh*.

She: I get restless with repetition.
I hear a tone and my mind gallivants.

September Light

It has no future but infinite charm
like an old actor in his last *Tempest*,
full of reflections.

*

A friend says human birth
is so improbable,
it must mean there is a more
spacious existence,
somewhere.

*

Somewhere on a hilltop, melting snows
meander among small mosses
and vultures sketch a cloudless sky.
There the dreamer relives her leaping days,
the pooling mists, and widening, slowing,
building-up alluvium
of a river wandering toward the sea.

*

Once you have seen the heron in the shallows,
the heron is always there.

JUDITH SLATER grew up in Brocton, NY, attended Alfred University and the University of North Carolina, and holds doctorates from Ohio State University (in English) and the University at Buffalo (in Clinical Psychology). She has taught at Canisius College and studied poetry under Irving Feldman and Carl Dennis, as well as in the Chautauqua Institute Literary Workshops. A finalist for both the MARGIE and *Passager* awards, she has had work featured in a number of journals and on Ted Kooser's national website, *American Life in Poetry*. She works as a psychologist and lives with her husband, a political scientist, in Williamsville, NY.

The not-for-profit **OUTRIDERS POETRY PROJECT** was founded in 1968 by Doug Eichhorn, Dan Murray and Max Wickert. With partial support from Poets & Writers and the New York State Council of the Arts, we have sponsored numerous readings, and have published work by writers living in, or significantly associated with, the Buffalo-Niagara region. Since 2010, we have been operating chiefly as a small press. Submissions for new books are considered each year between January 1 and April 15. For details check our website or write to:

Outriders Poetry Project
314 Highland Avenue
Buffalo, New York 14222
Email: maxwickert1@mac.com